Handwriting Practice Workbook

Children's Reading & Writing Education Books

PROFESSOR GUSTO
EDUCATIONAL & INFORMATIVE BOOKS FOR CHILDREN
(PRE-K / K-12)

Practice Writing (Words)

Trace and rewrite the the following words.

about

after

apple

away

baby

back

base

being

bike

cake

candy

child

deep

down

dress

each

egg

fall

farm

feet

first

floor

four

game

gave

glad

happy

hard

here

hope

inch

jump

king

know

land

last

left

live

love

made

met

mile

move

nail

name

nine

open

over

page

part

pay

post

rabbit

read

road

room

same

seen

seven

shoe

small

spell

store

teach

thank

that

them

there

they

thing

think

three

time

today

truck

very

walk

want

warm

week

well

went

what

when

while

white

who

why

wind

wish

with

woke

work

your

zoo

Practice Writing (Sentences)

Trace and rewrite the the following words.

This is a book.

I am a girl.

It is difficult.

It is ten o'clock.

I am thirsty.

It is getting dark.

I take a shower.

I brush my teeth.

I comb my hair.

I am eating.

Let us go!

Hurry up!

Hold on!

Very good!

www.ingramcontent.com/pod-product-compliance
Lightning Source LLC
LaVergne TN
LVHW082253070426
835507LV00034B/2275